IMAGES

of America

LOWELL

STATUE OF VICTORY.

The Ladd and Whitney Monument was erected in memory of Addison Whitney (who was twenty-two years old when he was killed) and Luther Ladd (who was seventeen), the first soldiers killed in the Civil War. Their bodies are buried beneath the monument. The statue of Winged Victory is a replica of one of the statues that stand outside the royal palace in Munich. It was a gift to the city from James C. Ayer, and stands near City Hall and the Ladd and Whitney Monument. (HG)

IMAGES
of America

LOWELL

John Pendergast

ARCADIA

First published 1996
Copyright © John Pendergast, 1996

ISBN 0-7524-0410-5

Published by Arcadia Publishing,
an imprint of the Chalford Publishing Corporation
One Washington Center, Dover, New Hampshire 03820
Printed in Great Britain

Library of Congress Cataloging-in-Publication Data applied for

The Boston Fish Market, at 80 Gorham Street, is probably the oldest extant business in Lowell. It is shown here *c*. 1920.

Contents

Acknowledgments

People who loaned their photographs for inclusion are credited at the end of each caption by their initials in parentheses.

I would like to thank the following: Esther Garland of the Dracut Historical Society for her tireless efforts on my behalf; Harvey Gagnon of the Dracut Historical Society for his support and fine example; Henry (Hank) Garrity, proprietor of H. Garrity Antiques, for the use of his extensive photographic collection (HG); the Lowell Arts Council and the Tyngsborough Arts Council for their financial assistance; Rick Boisvert for his painstaking efforts at the photo stand; Mitch Schulman, Paul Coppens, and Dave Ambrose at the South Campus Media Center; Mrs. Bacon and the staff and trustees of the Tyngsborough Town Library (TTL); Peter Alexis, keeper of the archival flame at the Lowell Memorial Library (PA); George Poirier of George's Photography of Lowell for the use of his extensive collection (GP); Guy Lefebvre of the Lowell Gallery (GL); Michael (Mac) MacDonagh (MM); Jerry Roth of Tyngsborough for the use of his extensive Harvard Brewery Collection (JR); Ray Clement of Riverbend Road, Tyngsborough (RC); Mehmet Ali; Paul Dunigan for the use of photographs from his collection (PD); Pat Pendergast of Riverbend Road, Tyngsborough (PP); James Keefe of Keefe Antiques (JK); Caitlin Pendergast for her technical and graphic assistance; Dr. Charles Nikolopoulos, Department of Philosophy, University of Massachusetts, Lowell (CN); Jack Flood of St. Patrick's Parish; David Shaughnessy, Lowell Police Department, retired (DS); Steven O'Connor for access to his family albums (SOC); Ciaran Pendergast for editorial assistance; Maire Pendergast for editorial assistance, coffee, and other means of sustenance; the Greek gentlemen at the Back Door for identification of some of the more obscure figures; Charles Panagiotakos, whose extensive Lowell postcard collection was most valuable (CP); Aida Panagiotakos for aid in identifying people in photographs; Betty Lou Sarris, Hidden Treasures Antiques, Tyngsborough (BLS); and the Fay-McCabe Funeral Home (FMF).

Material was also used from Cowley's 1862 *History of Lowell* and the 1894 *Illustrated History of Lowell*.

Introduction

"The Indians speak of a beautiful river far to the South, which they call Merrimac."

Sieur De Monts 1604

On June 17, 1605, a 15-ton bark entered the Merrimac River and sailed up to a point where it could be observed by the Wamesits and Pawtuckets, the native inhabitants of the land which over two hundred years later would be named Lowell. On board were Pierre du Gua, Sieur De Monts, a Huguenot aristocrat, his captain, Samuel de Champlain, a group of twenty sailors, a few French gentlemen, and an Indian guide, Panounias, and his wife. Pierre du Gua named the river for himself, Riviere du Gua, and proceeded on his survey of the New England coast. Champlain, recording the event, called it "a river of considerable magnitude."

Surely du Gua was not the first European to view the Merrimac, but he was the first to be recorded. Most likely, Basque, French, Spanish, Dutch, and English sailors had made their way to the Pawtucket Falls to trade with the natives that dwelled along the shores, especially in the spring, when they gathered to net the salmon which migrated to the place in vast numbers. In 1613, Captain John Smith sailed up the river, but made little mention of it except to call it by its original name, the one it has held since then with some spelling variations.

By the 1630s, with the coasts from Maine to Cape Cod having already been settled, people began exploring the area around Lowell. Passaconaway, the ruler of all the Native Americans from Canada to a few miles south of the Merrimac, surrendered his authority to the English governor, and in 1655 the fifteen families that had settled at Sunneanasset ("eel place") and Naamkeag ("fishing place") founded a town. They called it Chelmsford, after the birthplace of the town's minister.

A triangle of land extending from the Pawtucket Falls across to the Concord (Muskatequid), about a mile below its confluence with the Merrimac, was set aside by John Eliot, the first minister to the local natives, as their reserved land. A ditch was dug the entire length to mark the boundary. It is said that some of the traces of that ditch still exist, but no specific locations have been recorded or found. The natives who lived here were called the Wamesit, and up until the last century, the area was called Wamesit Neck. All of downtown Lowell, the Acre, Fort Hill, Edson Cemetery, and much more were in Wamesit Neck. The other local tribe was the Pawtucket, who lived on the other side of the river and had a major settlement at the Falls. In 1660, Passaconaway passed his authority to his second son, Wannalancet, who lived in the region of Concord, New Hampshire. The present-day McDonalds is located on the former site of Passaconaway's longhouse. In 1669, fearing a Mohawk attack, Wannalancet moved down to Wamesit with a large group of braves and built a fort on what would come to be known as Fort Hill. By 1674, about 275 natives still lived at Wamesit Neck; only 75 had been converted to Christianity.

In 1676, the settlers built a fort at Pawtucket Falls. Much of the land was purchased from the natives, usually for bolts of cloth, shirts, or kettles. The $24 purchase of Manhattan was a good deal for the natives in comparison to what they got for their land around Lowell.

By 1686, the natives were in a sorry state to say the least. The Mohawks, perennial enemies, were still after them, and the natives to the south distrusted them because they refused to partake in King Phillips War (1675–76), the last ditch effort to expel the colonists. The same war made them suspect to the colonists, who began to harass and kill them. In 1687 Wannalancet sold Wamesit Neck and other vast tracts of land to Thomas Henchman and Jonathan Tyng, and went to live 300 miles away, in the northernmost section of his realm, at the point where the St. Francis River meets the St. Lawrence River. Henchman and Tyng paid Wannalancet £150 for the 2,500 acres of Wamesit Neck. Fifty Chelmsford residents paid Tyng £50 each for one-fiftieth of one-half of the land; Tyng kept the rest for himself. His £150 investment netted him a profit of £2,000 plus 1,300 acres of prime farmland.

Those fifty Chelmsford residents settled or sold their purchases and the community of East Chelmsford was soon established. By 1725, the area became part of Chelmsford proper. Two years later, Chelmsford was hit by the worst earthquake in its history. Undaunted, the community continued to expand. A sawmill was established by John Ford at the point where the Merrimac and Concord meet, the present the site of Middlesex Community College. Ford had been at the siege of Fort Louisburg in 1746 and led a Chelmsford company at the Battle of Bunker Hill. The first bridge was built across the river in 1797 at the site of the present-day Pawtucket Bridge. It was a toll bridge, built entirely of wood. There has been a bridge on the site ever since.

At this time Lowell was still primarily a farming community, but the Merrimac was too powerful a force for things to remain pastoral. The Middlesex Canal, the first transport canal in the United States, was opened in 1804. It ran from Charlestown to a point in Middlesex Village not far from the present-day Hadley Field, where it dropped into the Merrimac. It was a major route until the arrival of the railroads. It finally ceased operations in 1854.

The story of the development of the mills and the part Lowell played in the Industrial Revolution as well as Lowell's waves of immigrants need not be repeated again here. There are several worthy treatises. Besides, this is not meant to be an academic work, but one created for sheer pleasure. It was not designed for the tourist, but for "Lowellians": those old-timers who'll recognize faces and places from the past, and newcomers to the city who wish to get an idea of what their community looked like before they arrived.

There will be scenes remembered and pleasantly recognized and, we hope, some amazement at the changes that have taken place. The corner of Broadway and Pawtucket Boulevard in the 1880s was unrecognizable to everyone we showed it to; great arguments and discussions arose over the location of particular shops and buildings in other photographs, or the occasion for a parade. Oftentimes there was no final resolution, but occasionally small signs or towers in the background shed light when examined by a loupe. Very frequently a close examination of a license plate dated an otherwise undateable photograph.

The pictures range from the 1860s to the 1960s, and with only a few exceptions (postcards mainly), they have never been published before. Throughout the community, private collections have been rifled. Trusting collectors have warily put their collections in my hands and wrung their own as I drove away with their treasures in the back of my car.

Sorting and cataloging presented unanticipated dilemmas. It was necessary to collect all the usable material before beginning the task of putting it in order. The first idea was to place everything in chronological order, but separating the shop fronts, parades, and the night life and social events into groups seemed more effective. Perhaps the most difficult decision was when to stop. There was always the chance that another excellent photograph would appear around the corner. I am quite sure that immediately after this book goes to the printer, several people will come forth with more photographic treasures. I hope you enjoy the ones contained herein.

One
Shops and Streets

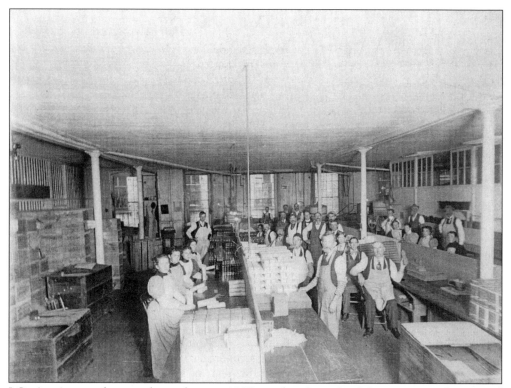

J.C. Ayer's manufactory, shown here *c.* 1885, produced much of the patent medicine used around the world. The faded sign painted many years ago on the factory on Middle Street can still be seen. Ayer's products earned unsolicited endorsements from the Pasha of Trebizond and the Emperor of China. Tsar Alexander invited him to his daughter's wedding. The company was founded in 1843 and employed over one hundred and fifty people. Among other ingredients, Ayer's company used 460,000 pounds of sugar yearly. (HG)

Charles T. Callahan's market was on Bridge Street. His brother Daniel had one on Suffolk Street, *c.* 1870. In 1870, there were 121 grocers in Lowell, along with 9 hotels, 99 boarding houses, 14 drugstores, 11 banks, 60 dressmakers, 13 photographers, 60 physicians, 14 horse stables, and 64 variety stores. (HG)

This Whipple Street market displays an enormous number of carcasses. The proprietor was J.H. Guinan, c. 1880. (HG)

The grocery store of John T. Connors was located at 141–43 Merrimack Street. (HG)

Michael McDonagh stands outside his grocery store on Tilden Street about 1900. This location is shown in the 1950s in a later photograph. (MM)

The corner of Cheever and Aiken Street was very much a French-Canadian community in 1891. The first shop on the left is the Lee Sun Laundry, at 37 Cheever Street; Pierre Messier owned a variety store at 33 Cheever Street, and Magasin de Coupons was at 29 Cheever Street. The Pharmacie Francaise was on the corner; Zoel St. Hilaire owned a variety store at 10 Aiken Street, and there was a barber shop at 16 Aiken Street.

Killpartrick Brothers Confectionery, at 176 Merrimack Street, is shown here with a crowd, c. 1886.

The Lawrence Street Cash Market was located at 364 Lawrence Street, c. 1900. (PD)

This is a view of Back Central Street looking towards Hosford Square, *c.* 1906. Some of these buildings still stand. (GP)

John J. Donnelly's blacksmith shop was at 285 Merrimack Street, *c.* 1870. (GP)

Napoleon Desmarais' hardware store, located at 778 Lakeview Avenue, is shown here *c.* 1910. It is presently the site of Ace Hardware. (GP)

O'Donnell's Dry Goods, at 184–86 Merrimack Street, advertised dry goods, cloaks, millinery, upholstery, kitchen furnishings, and bedding. This photograph was taken on the occasion of the employees' annual outing, 1910. (SOC)

Bailey's Drug Store, at 79 Merrimack Street, on the corner of John Street, was established in 1840. Its slogan was: "No candy, cigars, or soda, but everything in drugs." In 1931 there were forty-six druggists in Lowell. (GP)

Union National Bank, at 41 John Street, gets a new roof. The bags on the sidewalk contain pebbles which will be lifted by the crane on the roof. There is now a parking lot in place of the building on the left. (HG)

Two
Working

The crew of the 1,700-horsepower Boott Mills hydroelectric unit is shown here on March 2, 1923, cementing the penstock at its junction with the wheelcase. (RC)

The management of the Locks and Canals corporation was photographed on June 1, 1923. The Locks and Canals is a private corporation, formed in the 1790s and still in operation. It is the oldest extant corporation in the United States. The company regulates the flow of the Merrimac River, among other charges. From left to right are George Mansur, Henry Lundbaum, and Silas S. Kent. (RC)

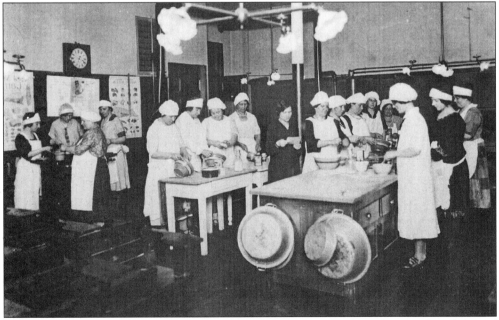

The Internation Institute on Palmer Street offered courses in sewing, cooking, and English, and helped immigrants to prepare for citizenship. It is shown here in the 1920s. (PDY)

The Daniel Gage Ice Company fleet was located on the present-day site of Sheehy Park on Pawtucket Boulevard. (PD)

Elbow of #5 Wheel
Boott Mills
Taken Sept. 27 1910
Crossing Merrimack
River.

The elbow above the Bridge Street bridge was manufactured at Lowell's Scannell Boiler Works, which was located on Tanner Street. This photograph was taken on September 27, 1910. (RC)

This is the same crew that appears in the photograph on p. 19. They are shown here in the process of installing the 1,700-horsepower Boott Mills hydroelectric unit on October 13, 1922. (RC)

The McKee Refridgerator [sic] Co. championship bowling team is shown here in 1935. The company was an attempt by the Daniel Gage Ice Company to keep pace with the modern world. (JK)

Mill girls in 1939 march on Market Street crossing the Northern Canal bridge approaching Dutton Street. (MM)

The ruins of the Pickering Hosiery Co. attest to devastation that fires often inflicted at the turn of the century. This fire occurred in 1888. (PD)

The Walkover Shoe Store was located on Merrimack Street in 1921. Later, this became the 20th Century Shoe Store. Note the swastikas in the windows. (HG)

Laundryman William Chin ran the Chinese laundry at 370 Central Street in 1931. At this time, there were eight laundries in Lowell run by men whose last names were Chin. In addition, there were six other Chinese laundries in Lowell run by non-Chins. (GP)

A new sign is being erected at Dufresne's Market, 253 Aiken Street, in the mid-1930s. The market closed in the mid-1950s. (GP)

Dickerman-McQuade's Clothing Store, at the corner of Market and Central Street, is shown here in the 1940s arrayed for Christmas. (GP)

Lowell Auto Supply was on Moody Street, across from the Passtime Club, next to Marie's Seafood Restaurant. George Fontaine is behind the counter and Henry Goulet is on the phone in this 1940s photograph. The area around Moody Street was very much a French-Canadian section of Lowell, and was previously known as "Little Canada." (GP)

Queena Flomp Traggis and Clementine Flomp Alexis are wicking at the Greek Candle Company, located at 32 Marion Street. Catherine Flomp wraps candles as Della Nicolopoulos looks on, *c*. 1948. (PA)

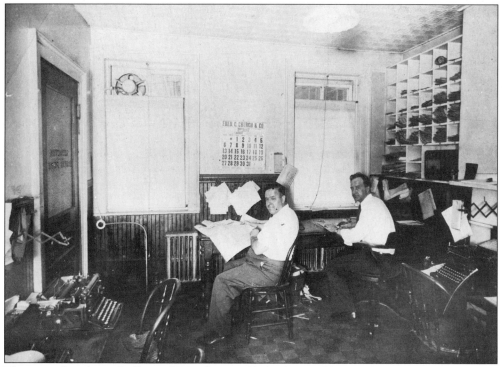

These are the editorial offices of *L'Etoile*, Lowell's leading and longest-lived French newspaper. In the center of this 1939 photograph is Antoine Clement, editor. (GP)

The Wannalancet Garage was located on Pawtucket Boulevard in the 1930s. Note the statue of Wannalancet over the door. (GP)

The first girder across the Northern Canal was lowered at 2:01 pm on September 13, 1894. (PD)

Gregory's Food Land was on Back Central Street. Viceroys were 27¢ a pack in the late 1950s. (GP)

Jack's Junk Yard was located on the Merrimac at Aiken Street. Note the Aiken Street bridge in the far right background. Roland Giguere sits on the hood, Killer Geoffroy is at the wheel, and Bob Heslin looks on in this 1930s photograph. (GP)

Tremblay's Piano Shop was on Moody Street in the late 1930s. (GP)

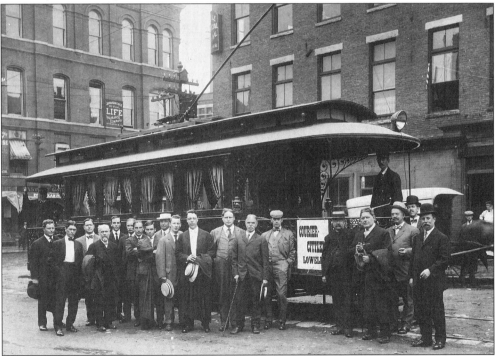

This Courier Citizen Outing took place *c*. 1910. (HG)

Three
Vehicles

This advertisement appeared in the 1870 Lowell Directory. (JP)

The "Lowell Vet" fire-fighting wagon is shown here in the 1880s. It was an antique even at that time. (PD)

Franklin Hook and Ladder Company No. 1 was photographed outside the headquarters of the Lowell Fire Department on Middle Street. In the 1870s there were eleven fire stations in Lowell. (GP)

This Daniel Gage ice delivery wagon was captured on film *c.* 1910. (PD)

A work crew lays tracks across the Northern Canal in 1894. (PD)

The "Paddy Wagon" is shown here *c.* 1906 outside the Market Street police station, now the home of the Colonial Gas Company. (PD)

This is a small portion of the Hood's Milk Company fleet of milk trucks. John Sullivan (uniformed) is in the center of this 1937 photograph. In the early 1930s there were seventeen milk dealers in Lowell. (GP)

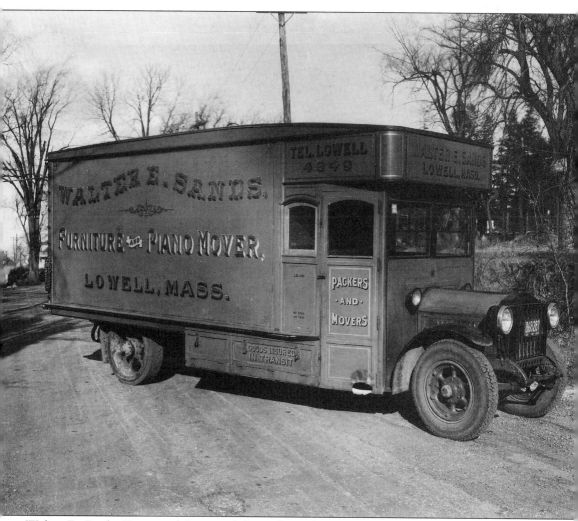

Walter E. Sands, Furniture Mover and Second Hand Furniture Dealer, was located at 205 Dutton Street in 1928. Mr. Sands lived on Westmeadow Road. The rear tires would encourage taking the good china in the sedan. In 1928 there were fifty-eight furniture dealers in Lowell. (GP)

Depot Taxi, telephone number 32, was located on Thorndike Street in the early 1930s. Their vehicles catered to the passengers disembarking from trains at the depot. (PD)

Fred Webster's plumbing shop on wheels is shown here at 167 D Street in the 1920s. (GP)

This Lavoie's Dairy delivery truck was photographed in 1935. Napoleon Lavoie's company was located at 515 Wilder Street. (HG)

A local delivery van from the Boott Mills is shown here in the 1930s. (PD)

This insurance photograph shows a 1946 Nash with a damaged right front fender. The adjoining green and cream car, reported to be the first two-tone car in Lowell, is a 1934 Hudson Terraplane Coupe. It was owned by Lowell photographer George Poirier. Note the antenna on the fender. (GP)

Four
People and Their Places

Passaconaway (*c.* 1580–1689), meaning "child of the bear," was the ruler of the local natives when Europeans arrived. His title was "bashaba," which translates roughly as "emperor"; he ruled from the Merrimac to the St. Lawrence and lived to be well over one hundred years old. His wigwam was on the site of the McDonalds on Pawtucket Boulevard. (Boutin's *History of Concord, NH.*)

Wannalancet, son of Passaconaway, was the last bashaba. His longhouse was on the site of the Franco-American School. He is shown with John Eliot, the first cleric in the greater Lowell community. (*Life of Elliot*, 1928.)

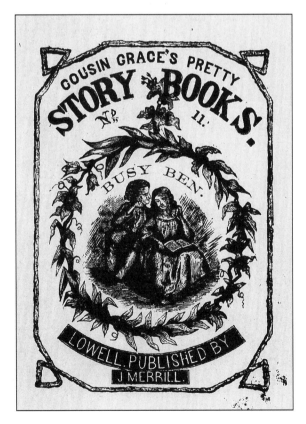

Busy Ben was published in Lowell in 1841. There were several printers and publishers in nineteenth-century Lowell. (JP)

This photograph was taken at George E. Mitchell's Gallery of Art on 89 Merrimack Street in the 1860s. The name of the lieutenant is unknown. The number of photography galleries in Lowell in the nineteenth century was surprisingly large. (JP)

The funeral services for Luther Ladd and Addison Whitney in Huntington Hall, in May 1861, were published in *Harpers* magazine. Another soldier was killed in the same skirmish, but his address could not be determined and he was ignored. (*Harpers.*)

This final group picture was taken in the mid-1890s on the beach at Liscannor, a tiny seaport in county Clare, on the west coast of Ireland. Sitting in the stern of the curragh is Anna Hayes. Kate Plunkett, with the buttons on her bodice, stands in the rear. Both women were coming to Lowell. Anna Hayes was the grandmother of retired Lowell Police Officer David Shaughnessy. (DS)

The corner of Broadway and Middlesex Streets is the location of the present-day Lowell Humane Society. Few people could recognize this location today, as it now includes the south campus of the University of Massachusetts, and Vulkor, the former General Electric plant. Colburn Hall (see p. 110) was erected in the early 1890s, so this picture is over one hundred years old. (GP)

These photographs show a military muster that occurred c. 1880s at the Parade Grounds on Gorham Street. There were four companies in Lowell. Their armories were in Market House. (HG)

These photographs, taken *c*. 1890 at the Lowell Photo Studios, show the wide range of effects it was possible to achieve through photography near the turn of the century. (JP)

A gathering of Greek women is shown here in the 1940s. (GP)

Anna Keefe and Babe Taylor are the maiden names of the two women in this 1933 photograph. (JP)

A day at Beaver Brook in Dracut meant fun and swimming lessons for the kids. Ricky Keefe (rear center) taught swimming to local kids. He was an Eastern Mass. bus driver and a champion swimmer who could dive into a hole in the frozen brook and swim out of another one 15 yards away. This is a *c.* 1935 photograph. (JP)

The fact that one of these "Centerville Belles" is male and dressed like a sailor seems to be of little importance. Centralville, often spelled Centerville, it was annexed to Lowell from Dracut in 1851. This photograph was taken on West Sixth Street in the 1920s. (JP)

John Hogan (left) immigrated to Lowell from county Sligo at the turn of the century. He became an Eastern Mass. bus driver and lived on West Sixth Street. George Keefe, his brother-in-law's brother, is on the right in this 1933 photograph. (JP)

Father Flaherty of St. Patricks presides at this gathering in 1926 of the officers of the Catholic Young Men's Lyceum. Jimmy McMullen is in the middle rear; John Murphy and future State Representative George T. Walsh are also in the group. (JP)

They Cut the Link That Dropped the Francis Gate

The heroes of Francis Gate, 1936, were captured in this photograph taken for the *Lowell Sun*. When the gate fell, much of the canal system was diverted from Lowell, which saved the area from a great deal of destruction.

This graduation at St. Joseph's Orphanage took place *c*. 1910. (GL)

Margaret Quinn thumbs her nose at an unknown suitor, *c.* 1907, at Rundlett's Court, Centralville. Her sister Marietta vamps in the background. (JP)

These loom-fixers worked at the Massachusetts Mills, *c.* 1910. Joseph Lefebvre (first row, sixth from the left) and his father (first row, seventh from the left) have been identified. (GL)

On May 25, 1923, this group of Greek men and boys posed for a photograph while on an outing. (CP)

Centralville kids are shown here, with a few Dracut ones mixed in. Tommy Keefe is in the first row on the left in this 1924 photograph. (JP)

Greek children playing in the Acre in the 1930s. (GP)

Emile Rondeau is getting out on the driver's side at the Alouette, just over the line into Dracut on Riverside Street. The Comedy Club is on the site today. The license plate on the car reads 1942. (GP)

The class officers of St. Patrick's in 1936 were, from left to right: John Callahan, Bill Gallagher, James O'Connor, and Reg Quinn. (SOC)

James O'Connor is in the front center of this 1936 photograph of eighth-grade graduates of St. Patrick's. (SOC)

Father Joe Denis was ably assisted by Sister Paul Etienne at First Communion at St. Jean d'Arc, 1932. (GP)

The Greek church officers posed for a photograph in the early 1930s. From left to right are: (front row) Mr. Sarris; Mr. Kohines, a coffee store owner; Mr. Costas Rodopoulos, an insurance agent, whose office was at 24 Merrimack Street; Mr. James Giavas, owner of Giavas Market at 436 Market Street; and Mr. Tsaffaras, the first Greek police officer in Lowell; (back row) Mr. James Karelas, owner of a novelty and dry goods store at 424 Market Street; and Mr. George Economou, a cigar manufacturer. (GP)

Breweries were among the earliest working groups to unionize; hence the odd early name for Lowell's well-known brewery. (GR)

The *Lowell Sun* newsboys meet Babe Ruth and Dizzy Dean in the late 1930s. (GP)

This funeral at the Holy Trinity Greek Orthodox Church occurred in the late 1930s. (CP)

Members of St. Patrick's Holy Name Society baseball team are shown here, *c*. 1936. (SOC)

The Hi-Hat Night Club was located at 600 Princeton Boulevard. This Hi-Hat employees' Christmas party took place in the late 1940s. (GP)

Jimmy Laverty, John Carney, Joey Arpin, Gary Boyle, Frank Keefe, and Jay Pendergast are among these faces at First Communion at St. Patrick's, 1946. (JP)

These Highland girls were photographed in 1940. From left to right are Ellen (Leahy) O'Connor, Pepsy Meehan, Harriet Smith, and Marilyn Leahy. (SOC)

The 1960 Bordeleau family reunion took place at the Passtime Club on Moody Street. (GP)

The first St. Jean d'Arc baseball team is shown here in 1936. Bobby Ayotte, to the right of Brother Frederick, went to the major leagues. (GP)

"Home from the war" was the caption under this photograph from the *Harvard Brewery Banner*. From left to right in this 1945 photograph are: Leo Garneau, Ernest Daigle, Victor Lepine, Paul Leblanc, Paul Thibodeau, and Raymond Boisvert. Leblanc flew 108 missions over China, Burma, and India. (GR)

On the reverse of this photograph is written: "My own play '33, A Musical Sketch," St. Joseph's Boy's School. From left to right in this 1933 photograph are: R. Martin, John Kerouac, Roger Drolet, J. Parent, and Eugene Lessard. (GP)

Jack Keefe (second row, fourth from the left), shown here in 1942, was only one of the many World War II heroes from greater Lowell. His destroyer earned the title, "the destroyer that fought like a battleship," but direct hits sank the ship during the Battle of Leyte Gulf, the largest naval battle in history. Keefe clung to the outside of a raft for fifty hours. Rear Admiral Robert Copeland, commander of the ship, announced before the battle that the ship was about to engage in "a fight against overwhelming odds from which survival could not be expected." Keefe became the postmaster at Dracut and was a well-known marathoner and musician. In a later photograph, he appears with his band. (*Lowell Sun*)

Bob Ayotte is shown here about eight years later with another Lowell boy, Skippy Roberge; both playing for the Boston Braves. Skippy was a second baseman who later coached at Keith Academy. Bob Ayotte is wearing the catcher's mitt in this mid-1940s photograph. (GP)

A War Bond march moves down Merrimack Street in the early 1940s. (HG)

Lowell High School girl officers march down Merrimack Street in 1942. (SOC)

These two views show a parade in 1930 as it moves up Merrimack Street. (HG)

Kearney Square was photographed in 1945 during VJ Day. Note the USO sign. Lee's Chop Suey is presently the Leahy Building, and Page's Clock is still a landmark. (GP)

The credit union group posed at the Bon Marche Department Store in the 1940s. Mildred Cate is at the bottom left; at the bottom center is Evelyn Cate, personnel manager. (BAS)

Father "Spike" Morrisette, a chaplain of the French Navy in America and a perennial parish priest at St. Jean d'Arc Parish, is shown here in 1950.

The Avon Cafe on Merrimack Street was photographed in 1950 on St. Patrick's Day. (JP)

Morse's Shoe Store was located at 130 Merrimack Street in the 1950s. (HG)

In town for the 1952 Fourth of July Parade, and parked across from the Lowell Sun building, the Kent County, Rhode Island Post 1144 tram engine was considered to be the most ornate in the country. (HG)

This photograph of 137 Hovey Street was taken *c.* 1890. (HG)

The triangular building in this *c.* 1905 postcard view of Central and Prescott Streets was torn down in the 1960s and replaced by a vacant lot. (CP)

City Hall is shown here in this late 1930s postcard view. Moody Street, on the right, is now totally gone. (CP)

In 1931 there were fifty separate businesses which had offices in the Central Block, located at 53 Central Street. (CP)

Tower's Corner and Central Street are shown here at the turn of the century. (CP)

This 1905 postcard view shows the Canal Walk along the Merrimac. (JP)

The YMCA was founded on February 4, 1867, on Back Central Street. It is shown here c. 1907. (CN)

The YMCA was at the corner of Merrimack and Dutton Streets, c. 1915. The building was razed in the 1960s. The canal flows under an arched vault, which was formerly underneath the building, but is presently exposed. (CP)

The State Armory on Westford Street was torn down in the early 1970s. The building was constructed of dark red sandstone, ornately carved in some places. The area is presently a vacant lot and parking area. (JP)

A. M. D. G.

➤ GRAND AND SOLEMN CEREMONY ◄

OF THE

Consecration of St. Patrick's Church

LOWELL, MASS.

Dedicated October 31, A. D. 1854; Rev. John O'Brien Pastor.
Consecrated September 7, A. D. 1879, Most Rev. John J. Williams, Archbishop of Boston, Consecrator.
Rev. Michael O'Brien, Pastor. 1st Assistant, Rev. Wm. O'Brien; 2nd Assistant, Rev. Wm. M. O'Brien; 3d Assistant, Rev. James Campbell.

Admit *Boyle Mary*

This Ticket is not Transferable.

North Transept.

Pew No. 6

This 1879 ticket of admission was to the consecration of the new St. Patrick's Church, which replaced the 1854 church building after it was destroyed by fire. (JP)

75

Merrimack Street and Lieutenant Paul T. Kearney Square can be seen in this view from East Merrimack Street. The Leahy Building in the right foreground still stands; in 1900, it was the home of the Lowell Commercial College. (CP)

Lowell firemen march down Gorham Street towards Central Street. Some of the buildings in this *c.* 1920 photograph still stand. (PD)

Central Street is shown here in the 1880s. (CP)

This is Central Street three decades later, in 1909. (CP)

The Colonial Building still stands at the corner of Merrimack and Central Streets. It presently houses the Dunkin Donuts on the corner, and is shown here in 1900. (CP)

City Hall is shown here in 1900 in a view looking toward Monument Square. (CP)

The Durkee Mansion, on Ferry Lane (which runs between Varnum Avenue and Pawtucket Boulevard), was the first house built on the Pawtucketville side of the river, *c.* 1660. It survived Indian raids and was a tavern and meetinghouse during the Revolutionary War. It was burned down in the mid-1950s. The vacant site is next to the firehouse and across from the Elks Club. (IHL)

This etching shows the first bridge across the Merrimac at Lowell, at the present-day site of the Pawtucket Bridge. Built by Parker Varnum of Dracut, it was the first of several bridges at this location. It was built entirely of wood, and was demolished in 1805 when a new one with stone piers and abutments was put in its place at a cost of $14,000. The second bridge remained a toll bridge until 1860. (CHL)

A funeral procession on Lawrence Street passes Moore Street in 1893. (FMF)

Five

Recreation and Night Life

The new Cadet Orchestra in 1904 consisted of the following: Louis Weiler (violin), worked for Fleischmann Yeast Co.; Richard Noonan (piano), lived at 115 Pleasant Street; James Buckley (cornet), lived at 3 Fletcher Street and was a retail tobacconist with a shop at 131 Central Street; Edward Looney (clarinetist), a tailor, owned a shop at 127 Central Street with H.W. Barnes; Stephen Kelty (drums and xylophone soloist); Thomas Gleason (trombone); Frank Mussey (flute and piccolo); Albert Shaw (cornet); and James McManus (prompter). Music was furnished for balls, parties, and receptions. (PA)

Lightweight boxer Paul Frechette, "The Blond Tiger," is shown here in the 1940s. He was very fast, but couldn't hit hard. (GP)

Jack Lemire threw the deadly punch at this outdoor sports night at St. Jean d'Arc in the 1950s, but John Falta, who is on the floor, was redeemed—he won megabucks later in life. (GP)

The singer of this wartime orchestra is Horace Cate from Crowley Street in the Grove. His brother Edward is the guitarist. Note that all the men are in uniform in this photograph from the early 1940s. (BLS)

The Jack Keefe Orchestra is shown here in the early 1960s, playing at the Idle Hour in Graniteville. The saxophonist also appears earlier as a naval hero of World War II. He was still running in the Boston Marathon in his sixties. With him are Gerry Bernier on bass, Hank Horman on piano, and Charlie Grondine on drums. (GP)

In the 1940s the Laurier Club was "The Busiest Spot Within 25 Miles." It was a "Smart Dine and Dance Club Featuring Novelty Entertainment," with no cover or minimum and two floor shows nightly. (CP)

Nick's Happy Hour was in Tyngsborough, but it was a familiar spot to many Lowellians. Gora's exotic stone dungeon was located downstairs in the 1940s. (CP)

The Nectar Lounge at 17 Market Street had air conditioning in the 1940s. (JP)

This 1940s photograph shows the interior of the Laconia Restaurant on Merrimack Street, "Lowell's Most Beautiful Bar." (JP)

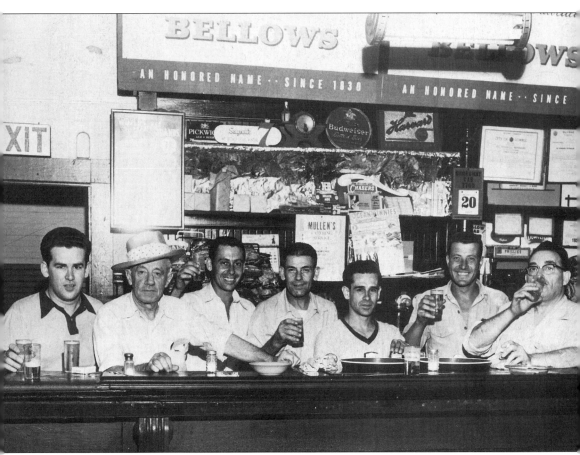

Donohue's Cafe was on the corner of Broadway and Willie Streets. From left to right, in this 1950s photograph, are: Ray Desjardins, "La Vigne de Brodeur" (avec chapeau); Leo Poirier; his father Joseph; Armand and Jerry Soucy; and George, the owner. We're not sure of George's last name. (GP)

The East End Cafe was at 15 West Fourth Street. Danny Critchard, Hank Golden, and Johnnie Golden were behind the bar in 1944. (JR)

The production department of the Harvard Eight Hour Brewing Company was 100% mustachioed in 1901. Breweries were the first businesses in the U.S. to become unionized because labor reform had become very successful in Germany and the immigrant brewers followed the practice—hence the "Eight Hour" in the original name of the well-known Lowell Brewery. (JR)

This 1944 photograph shows a night out at the Moulin Rouge. From left to right are: Irene Mitchell, Joseph Pendergast, Ann Pendergast, and popular local entertainer Manny Diaz. (JP)

These revelers were photographed on New Years Eve, 1950, at Contakos' Cafe. From left to right are: Peter Flomp, Catherine Flomp (seen wrapping candles in an earlier picture), Jimmy Contakos, Sophie Pappas, Dan Pappas, Lorraine Nicolopoulos, and Nick Contakos. (PA)

James Vacoulas owned the Cosmopolitan Cafe on Market Street. He is shown here in 1944 with John Rowan, his bartender. (JR)

The Hi-Hat Night Club was located at 600 Princeton Boulevard. This Hi-Hat employees' Christmas party took place in the late 1940s. (GP)

The Five "J"s gave Lowell its first taste of "The Devil's Music." In this early 1960s photograph are: Bucky Auger (guitar); Lou Murray (bongos); Bob Knoop (drums); Huck Finneral (conga and vocals); Arthur Leblanc (bass); and Ray Lessard (guitar). (GP)

Six
More People, Places, and Vehicles

In this photograph of Harry Truman's whistle-stop in Lowell are Attorneys Richard and Joseph Donohue, Mayor Henry Beaudry, Governor Paul Dever (behind the mayor), Senator John Kennedy, Maurice Tobin, Hubert McGloughlin, and Paul Lappin. (GP)

The City of Lights Committee assembled on the steps of City Hall in the 1950s. (GP)

Well-organized auto races were held annually soon after the turn of the century along Pawtucket Boulevard. Another familiar course, shown here *c.* 1906, ran from Varnum Avenue to Sherburne Avenue in Tyngsborough. (TTL)

Racing cars flash past spectators along the course. (TTL)

The racers are shown here passing the Tyngsborough Country Club. (TTL)

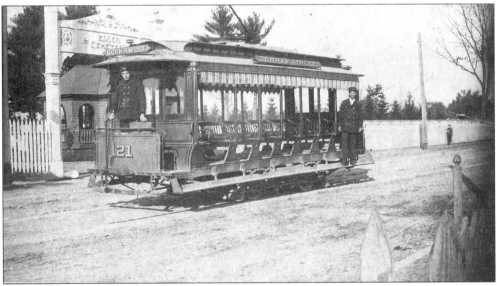

This car is very much like those in Lowell today. It is shown passing the Edson Cemetery, a regular stop on the Gorham Street line, *c.* 1910. (PD)

These are two early views of the Middlesex Canal. The above photograph is of an oil painting. The bridge on the left crosses the canal, and the dirt road leading off to the left would eventually become Middlesex Street. The exact location of the drawing below has proven impossible to determine. (JP)

Type of scows used on the old Middlesex Canal.
From Boston to Lowell.   Years, 1804 to 1852.

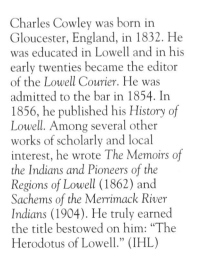

Robert B. Caverly, a resident of Centralville, was a lawyer and poet. In 1866, Caverly published *The Merrimac and its Incidents*, an epic poem, both in style and length. To quote the poem:

> "Thus at creation's dawn did Merrimac
> Begin to flow. The storm subsides, and *light*,
> Bright gleaming sunbeams, broke from sable night.
> And now the sweeping wave, with banks o'erflown,
> *Brilliant* and *grand* 'mid azure splendor shone,
> Roll on . . ." (JP)

Charles Cowley was born in Gloucester, England, in 1832. He was educated in Lowell and in his early twenties became the editor of the *Lowell Courier*. He was admitted to the bar in 1854. In 1856, he published his *History of Lowell*. Among several other works of scholarly and local interest, he wrote *The Memoirs of the Indians and Pioneers of the Regions of Lowell* (1862) and *Sachems of the Merrimack River Indians* (1904). He truly earned the title bestowed on him: "The Herodotus of Lowell." (IHL)

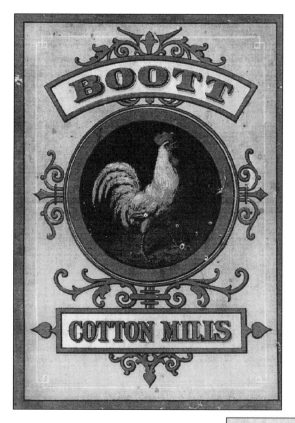

The rooster became the trademark of the Boott Mills and was used on advertising and labeling. This is a copy of an early label for cloth bolts, *c*. 1850. (JP)

Father Michael O'Brien was the pastor of the new church at St. Patrick Parish in 1854. He was born in 1825 in Ballina, county Tipperary, Ireland. (IHL)

St. Patrick's Church on Suffolk Street was the first Irish, hence Catholic, church north of Boston. This engraving is of the second church on the site, consecrated in October 1854. The first, a wooden structure, burned to the ground. On the left of the church is the rectory; on the right is the boys and the girls schools. (JP)

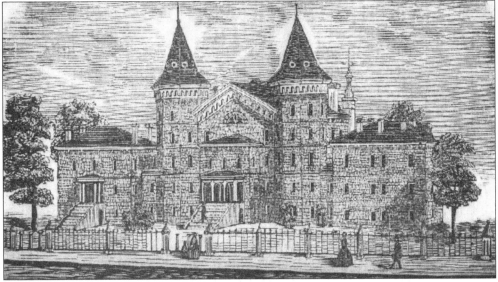

The Middlesex County Jail on Thorndike Street was erected in 1856 and cost about $150,000. The architect of the original was Lowell native James H. Rand. Cowley, in his *History of Lowell*, states: "The senseless manner in which the county commissioners wasted the people's money on this jail, brought the "ring" which has so long controlled our county affairs into disrepute." When the jail became Keith Academy in the 1920s the cells were transformed into classrooms and the exercise yards became football fields. The conversion was directed by another Lowell architect, Henry Rourke, who also built Lowell High. (Cowley's *History of Lowell*)

This crowd awaits a parade outside the county courthouse on Gorham Street in the 1870s. Notice the picket fence in the foreground, indicating that St. Peter's Church had not yet been erected. (JP)

A circle of stones on Druid Hill in Leblanc Park, off Westmeadow Road, is remarkably correlative to stone circles from the Bronze Age in northwestern Europe. Excavated in 1984, no pre-Columbian origins were determined, but the issue is still unresolved in the minds of some scholars. (JP)

The Coburn Mission was erected *c.* 1822 on Varnum Avenue, on the site of an earlier school, which was built in the 1750s. The mission building remained a school for over one hundred years. It stood for decades after it ceased to be used; children enjoyed playing with the eighteenth-century harpsichord that it housed, and at one point two-hundred-year-old schoolbooks were found rotting inside. It was finally razed in the early 1960s. (GP)

This photograph shows 190 Branch Street in the 1950s. (CP)

Bridge Street is under water, in this view looking toward Merrimack Street in 1936. (GP)

George Vozeolas' drug store was located at 523 Market Street in the 1930s. (CN)

Vaios Coravos' market was at 153 Broadway in the 1930s. (CN)

Edwin Poitras of 52 Nottingham Street is shown here being rewarded the Navy Cross. He was parachuted into Nazi-controlled France one month before D-Day to operate a radio with the French resistance forces. "One day as I was getting some cigarettes I was chased by the Gestapo, who started to fire submachine guns from their car. I quickly drew a phosphorous grenade from my pocket and threw it out of the speeding car I was in. The Germans, seeing I had thrown something from the car stopped quickly. Their misfortune was to stop completely over the grenade as it touched the ground. In a few minutes, their car with four very dead Gestapo men was destroyed, making possible my getaway." (GR)

The Holy Trinity Greek Orthodox Church was located at 107 Jefferson Street in the 1930s. Note the buildings behind the church; the housing project now stands on the site. (CN)

Sarris Market was located at 439 Market Street. The owners of the store, Costos and Vasila Sarris, lived at 420 Market Street in the 1930s. (CN)

This early Greek Revival house, built at 261–67 Worthen Street in the early decades of the nineteenth century, was inhabited mostly by Greeks one hundred years later. Some of the inhabitants included the Georgopoulos, Dabalis, Gekas, Mangroutsas, Kretsas, MacPhillips, Gocas, and Chandikas families. (CN)

The Panagiotopoulas Building on Adams Street is shown here in the late 1920s. This building still stands. (CN)

Charlies Variety was located at 570–80 Market Street in the 1930s. Notice the poster for the Royal Theatre in the window. (CN)

This grocery store, located at 1–3 Little Street, belonged to John Maniatakos. In 1931, every family living on the street was Greek. Like much of the Greek portion of the Acre, the street was eliminated when the housing project was constructed in the late 1930s. (CN)

The corner of Adams and Market Streets is shown here in the early 1930s, before the building of the housing project. (CN)

Eddie O'Connor's Orchestra played at the Commodore Ballroom in the 1950s. (SOC)

The Hildreth Building was located on Merrimack Street, *c.* 1885. The Freewill Baptist Church, erected 1834 at a cost of $20,000, most of which was paid by mill girls, was previously on this site. The church ultimately was purchased by Ben Butler and Fisher Hildreth, who converted it into a theatre and museum. Over the course of a nine-year period, it was struck by lightning and burned three separate times. In 1856 it was converted into a dance hall, a bowling alley, legal offices, and a newspaper. Lola Montez, the mistress of the King of Bavaria, gave a lecture on "Beautiful Women" at this spot. (GL)

The Freewill Baptist Church is shown here in an etching from Cowley's *History of Lowell* (1862).

The Torrent Engine House was located on Branch Street, *c.* 1890. The building still exists. (GP)

Lowell Normal School on Broadway, shown here in 1894, is now Coburn Hall on the south campus of the University of Massachusetts, Lowell. Note the absence of any other college buildings.

Palmer Street is shown here in the 1930s. (GP)

This fire occurred at the Armory on Middle Street, probably during the 1880s. (GP)

This *c.* 1906 photograph was taken by someone looking down Market Street from Central Street. (GP)

The Bon Marche Department Store on Merrimack Street is shown here after a rainstorm in the 1930s. (GP)

This is the Boston and Maine Railway station on Central Street, *c.* 1876. Later, this building held the Rialto Theatre, the Marathon Shoe Shine Parlor, and other businesses. It is presently under reconstruction. (GP)

The Tap Room at the Harvard Brewery on Plain Street is shown here, *c.* 1912. (GP)

Henry Gienandt (left foreground) and former coopers Jack Lawler and Herman Boehm can be seen in this 1907 photograph of a corner of the cooperage shop at the Harvard Brewery. Henry Thumm is on the extreme right. (GP)

A remarkably quiet Merrimack Street was captured in this photograph dating from the 1890s. (GP)

The Colonial Building on the corners of Central and Merrimack Streets is shown here in the 1920s, just before the opening of a new five and ten cent store. Most of the buildings in this picture still exist. (GP)

This interior shot of the Suffolk Knitting Mills was taken in the 1940s. (GP)

The mansion of J.C. Ayer was built on the site of Wannalancet's longhouse, which stood here in the late seventeenth century. The cast iron fence surrounding the building was brought back from New Orleans by Benjamin Butler after the Civil War. The wife of General George S. Patton was born in this house. It presently houses the Franco-American School. Notice the absence of any of the additions which now surround it. It is shown here in the 1880s. (GP)

The Pawtucketville School, located on Mammoth Road, is shown in the mid-1920s.

This is a gathering of the Centralville Social Club in the 1920s. The club was, and still is, located on Lakeview Avenue. (GP)

Lowell's leading lady, Bette Davis, receives tribute from her local public at the Auditorium in the 1950s. (GP)

The junction of Gorham and Central Streets is shown here in the 1870s. F.H. Butler's apothecary shop is on the corner. (PD)

This postcard of Shedd Park is postmarked 1907. (CP)

George W. Healey's embalming parlor was located at 8 Merrimack Square in the 1880s. The wagon outside is a flower delivery truck from Morse and Beals Florists. (PD)

Engine Company No. 6 was located at 467 Fletcher Street, in what is now the Lafayette Club. This is a *c.* 1890 photograph. (GP)

Townsfolk meander about after a parade on Merrimack Street in the 1870s. (JP)

C.I. Hood's patent medicine laboratories and manufactory, shown here *c.* 1870, was located on Thorndike Street. Hood's production was dwarfed only by Lowell's other patent medicine magnate, J.C. Ayer.

This 1910 postcard shows Central Bridge crossing Bridge Street, looking toward Kearney Square. (CP)

Central Bridge is shown here in 1861. (IHL)